T0124689

A LETTER FROM LI PO  AND OTHER POEMS

A

LETTER

FROM

 Li Po

AND OTHER POEMS

BY CONRAD AIKEN

NEW YORK • OXFORD UNIVERSITY PRESS

1955

Copyright 1954, 1955 by Conrad Aiken
© Conrad Aiken, 1955
Library of Congress Catalogue Card Number: 55-9706


Printed in the United States of America

# CONTENTS

44046

1

NOTE

In 'A Letter from Li Po,' as anyone familiar with the poetry of Li Po will soon perceive, I have quoted or paraphrased a few passages from the work of that great Chinese poet of the eighth century, as I have drawn on some of the circumstances of his life. Of particular use to me in this have been the beautiful translations of Li Po by Shigeyoshi Obata, *The Works of Li Po*, with his illuminating preface, and *The Poetry and Career of Li Po*, by Arthur Waley. Of use to me also was Herbert A. Giles's *Chinese Literature*. I must also acknowledge indebtedness to a review of Jean Tardieu by Marcel Arland in *La Nouvelle Revue Francaise* (April, 1953) for other notes and notions. And further, not only in the Li Po poem but in one or two others I have found very suggestive Peter Goffin's brilliant book, *The Realm of Art*.

I

Fanfare of northwest wind, a bluejay wind
announces autumn, and the Equinox
rolls back blue bays to a far afternoon.
Somewhere beyond the Gorge Li Po is gone,
looking for friendship or an old love's sleeve
or writing letters to his children, lost,
and to his children's children, and to us.
What was his light? of lamp or moon or sun?
Say that it changed, for better or for worse,
sifted by leaves, sifted by snow; on mulberry silk
a slant of witch-light; on the pure text
a slant of genius; emptying mind and heart
for winecups and more winecups and more words.
What was his time? Say that it was a change,
but constant as a changing thing may be,
from chicory's moon-dark blue down the taut scale
to chicory's tenderest pink, in a pink field
such as imagination dreams of thought.
But of the heart beneath the winecup moon
the tears that fell beneath the winecup moon
for children lost, lost lovers, and lost friends,
what can we say but that it never ends?
Even for us it never ends, only begins.

Yet to spell down the poem on her page,
margining her phrases, parsing forth
the sevenfold prism of meaning, up the scale
from chicory pink to blue, is to assume
Li Po himself: as he before assumed
the poets and the sages who were his.
Like him, we too have eaten of the word:
with him are somewhere lost beyond the Gorge:
and write, in rain, a letter to lost children,
a letter long as time and brief as love.

And yet not love, not only love. Not caritas
or only that. Nor the pink chicory love,
deep as it may be, even to moon-dark blue,
in which the dragon of his meaning flew
for friends or children lost, or even
for the beloved horse, for Li Po's horse:
not these, in the self's circle so embraced:
too near, too dear, for pure assessment: no,
a letter crammed and creviced, crannied full,
storied and stored as the ripe honeycomb
with other faith than this.
                                        As of sole pride
and holy loneliness, the intrinsic face
worn by the always changing shape between
end and beginning, birth and death.
How moves that line of daring on the map?
Where was it yesterday, or where this morning
when thunder struck at seven, and in the bay
the meteor made its dive, and shed its wings,
and with them one more Icarus? Where struck
that lightning-stroke which in your sleep you saw
wrinkling across the eyelid? Somewhere else?
But somewhere else is always here and now.

Each moment crawls that lightning on your eyelid:
each moment you must die. It was a tree
that this time died for you: it was a rock
and with it all its local web of love:
a chimney, spilling down historic bricks:
perhaps a skyful of Ben Franklin's kites.
And with them, us. For we must hear and bear
the news from everywhere: the hourly news,
infinitesimal or vast, from everywhere.

Sole pride and loneliness: it is the state
the kingdom rather of all things: we hear
news of the heart in weather of the Bear,
slide down the rungs of Cassiopeia's Chair,
still on the nursery floor, the Milky Way;
and, if we question one, must question all.
What is this 'man'? How far from him is 'me'?
Who, in this conch-shell, locked the sound of sea?
We are the tree, yet sit beneath the tree,
among the leaves we are the hidden bird,
we are the singer and are what is heard.
What is this 'world'? Not Li Po's Gorge alone,
and yet, this too might be. 'The wind was high
north of the White King City, by the fields
of whistling barley under cuckoo sky,'
where, as the silkworm drew her silk, Li Po
spun out his thoughts of us. 'Endless as silk'
(he said) 'these poems for lost loves, and us,'
and, 'for the peachtree, blooming in the ditch.'
Here is the divine loneliness in which
we greet, only to doubt, a voice, a word,
the smoke of a sweetfern after frost, a face
touched, and loved, but still unknown, and then
a body, still mysterious in embrace.

Taste lost as touch is lost, only to leave
dust on the doorsill or an ink-stained sleeve:
and yet, for the inadmissible, to grieve.
Of leaf and love, at last, only to doubt:
from world within or world without, kept out.

IV

Caucus of robins on an alien shore
as of the Ho-Ho birds at Jewel Gate
southward bound and who knows where and never late
or lost in a roar at sea. Rovers of chaos
each one the 'Rover of Chao,' whose slight bones
shall put to shame the swords. We fly with these,
have always flown, and they
stay with us here, stand still and stay,
while, exiled in the Land of Pa, Li Po
still at the Wine Spring stoops to drink the moon.
And northward now, for fall gives way to spring,
from Sandy Hook and Kitty Hawk they wing,
and he remembers, with the pipes and flutes,
drunk with joy, bewildered by the chance
that brought a friend, and friendship, how, in vain,
he strove to speak, 'and in long sentences,' his pain.
Exiled are we. Were exiles born. The 'far away,'
language of desert, language of ocean, language of sky,
as of the unfathomable worlds that lie
between the apple and the eye,
these are the only words we learn to say.
Each morning we devour the unknown. Each day
we find, and take, and spill, or spend, or lose,
a sunflower splendor of which none knows the source.

15

This cornucopia of air! This very heaven
of simple day! We do not know, can never know,
the alphabet to find us entrance there.
So, in the street, we stand and stare,
to greet a friend, and shake his hand,
yet know him beyond knowledge, like ourselves;
ocean unknowable by unknowable sand.

V

The locust tree spills sequins of pale gold
in spiral nebulae, borne on the Invisible
earthward and deathward, but in change to find
the cycles to new birth, new life. Li Po
allowed his autumn thoughts like these to flow,
and, from the Gorge, sends word of Chouang's dream.
Did Chouang dream he was a butterfly?
Or did the butterfly dream Chouang? If so,
why then all things can change, and change again,
the sea to brook, the brook to sea, and we
from man to butterfly; and back to man.
This 'I,' this moving 'I,' this focal 'I,'
which changes, when it dreams the butterfly,
into the thing it dreams of; liquid eye
in which the thing takes shape, but from within
as well as from without: this liquid 'I':
how many guises, and disguises, this
nimblest of actors takes, how many names
puts on and off, the costumes worn but once,
the player queen, the lover, or the dunce,
hero or poet, father or friend,
suiting the eloquence to the moment's end;
childlike, or bestial; the language of the kiss

sensual or simple; and the gestures, too,
as slight as that with which an empire falls,
or a great love's abjured; these feignings, sleights,
savants, or saints, or fly-by-nights,
the novice in her cell, or wearing tights
on the high wire above a hell of lights:
what's true in these, or false? which is the 'I'
of 'I's'? Is it the master of the cadence, who
transforms all things to a hoop of flame, where through
tigers of meaning leap? And are these true,
the language never old and never new,
such as the world wears on its wedding day,
the something borrowed with something chicory blue?
In every part we play, we play ourselves;
even the secret doubt to which we come
beneath the changing shapes of self and thing,
yes, even this, at last, if we should call
and dare to name it, we would find
the only voice that answers is our own.
We are once more defrauded by the mind.

Defrauded? No. It is the alchemy by which we grow.
It is the self becoming word, the word
becoming world. And with each part we play
we add to cosmic *Sum* and cosmic sum.
Who knows but one day we shall find,
hidden in the prism at the rainbow's foot,
the square root of the eccentric absolute,
and the concentric absolute to come.

## VI

The thousand eyes, the Argus 'I's' of love,
of these it was, in verse, that Li Po wove
the magic cloak for his last going forth,
into the Gorge for his adventure north.
What is not seen or said? The cloak of words
loves all, says all, sends back the word
whether from Green Spring, and the yellow bird
'that sings unceasing on the banks of Kiang,'
or 'from the Green Moss Path, that winds and winds,
nine turns for every hundred steps it winds,
up the Sword Parapet on the road to Shuh.'
'Dead pinetrees hang head-foremost from the cliff.
The cataract roars downward. Boulders fall
splitting the echos from the mountain wall.
No voice, save when the nameless birds complain,
in stunted trees, female echoing male;
or, in the moonlight, the lost cuckoo's cry,
piercing the traveller's heart. Wayfarer from afar,
why are you here? what brings you here? why here?'

VII

Why here. Nor can we say why here. The peachtree bough
scrapes on the wall at midnight, the west wind
sculptures the wall of fog that slides
seaward, over the Gulf Stream.
                                                    The rat
comes through the wainscot, brings to his larder
the twinned acorn and chestnut burr. Our sleep
lights for a moment into dream, the eyes
turn under eyelids for a scene, a scene,
O and the music, too, of landscape lost.
And yet, not lost. For here savannahs wave
cressets of pampas, and the kingfisher
binds all that gold with blue.
                                            Why here? why here?
Why does the dream keep only this, just this—?
Yes, as the poem or the music do?


The timelessness of time takes form in rhyme:
the lotus and the locust tree rehearse
a four-form song, the quatrain of the year:
not in the clock's chime only do we hear
the passing of the Now into the past,

the passing into future of the Now:
but in the alteration of the bough
time becomes visible, becomes audible,
becomes the poem and the music too:
time becomes still, time becomes time, in rhyme.
Thus, in the Court of Aloes, Lady Yang
called the musicians from the Pear Tree Garden,
called for Li Po, in order that the spring,
tree-peony spring, might so be made immortal.
Li Po, brought drunk to court, took up his brush,
but washed his face among the lilies first,
then wrote the song of Lady Flying Swallow:
which Hsuang Sung, the emperor, forthwith played,
moving quick fingers on a flute of jade.
Who will forget that afternoon? Still, still,
the singer holds his phrase, the rising moon
remains unrisen. Even the fountain's falling blade
hangs in the air unbroken, and says: Wait!

Text into text, text out of text. Pretext
for scholars or for scholiasts. The living word
springs from the dying, as leaves in spring
spring from dead leaves, our birth from death.
And all is text, is holy text. Sheepfold Hill
becomes its name for us, and yet is still
unnamed, unnamable, a book of trees
before it was a book for men or sheep,
before it was a book for words. Words, words,
for it is scarlet now, and brown, and red,
and yellow where the birches have not shed,
where, in another week, the rocks will show.
And in this marriage of text and thing how can we know
where most the meaning lies? We climb the hill
through bullbriar thicket and the wild rose, climb
past poverty-grass and the sweet-scented bay
scaring the pheasant from his wall, but can we say
that it is only these, through these, we climb,
or through the words, the cadence, and the rhyme?
Chang Hsu, calligrapher of great renown,
needed to put but his three cupfuls down
to tip his brush with lightning. On the scroll,
wreaths of cloud rolled left and right, the sky

opened upon Forever. Which is which?
The poem? Or the peachtree in the ditch?
Or is all one? Yes, all is text, the immortal text,
Sheepfold Hill the poem, the poem Sheepfold Hill,
and we, Li Po, the man who sings, sings as he climbs,
transposing rhymes to rocks and rocks to rhymes.
The man who sings. What is this man who sings?
And finds this dedicated use for breath
for phrase and periphrase of praise between
the twin indignities of birth and death?
Li Yung, the master of the epitaph,
forgetting about meaning, who himself
had added 'meaning' to the book of 'things,'
lies who knows where, himself sans epitaph,
his text, too, lost, forever lost . . .

                              And yet, no,
text lost and poet lost, these only flow
into that other text that knows no year.
The peachtree in the poem is still here.
The song is in the peachtree and the ear.

The winds of doctrine blow both ways at once.
The wetted finger feels the wind each way,
presaging plums from north, and snow from south.
The dust-wind whistles from the eastern sea
to dry the nectarine and parch the mouth.
The west wind from the desert wreathes the rain
too late to fill our wells, but soon enough,
the four-day rain that bears the leaves away.
Song with the wind will change, but is still song
and pierces to the rightness in the wrong
or makes the wrong a rightness, a delight.
Where are the eager guests that yesterday
thronged at the gate? Like leaves, they could not stay,
the winds of doctrine blew their minds away,
and we shall have no loving-cup tonight.
No loving-cup: for not ourselves are here
to entertain us in that outer year,
where, so they say, we see the Greater Earth.
The winds of doctrine blow our minds away,
and we are absent till another birth.

X

Beyond the Sugar Loaf, in the far wood,
under the four-day rain, gunshot is heard
and with the falling leaf the falling bird
flutters her crimson at the huntsman's foot.
Life looks down at death, death looks up at life,
the eyes exchange the secret under rain,
rain all the way from heaven: and all three
know and are known, share and are shared, a silent
moment of union and communion.

                             Have we come
this way before, and at some other time?
Is it the Wind Wheel Circle we have come?
We know the eye of death, and in it too
the eye of god, that closes as in sleep,
giving its light, giving its life, away:
clouding itself as consciousness from pain,
clouding itself, and then, the shutter shut.
And will this eye of god awake again?
Or is this what he loses, loses once,
but always loses, and forever lost?
It is the always and unredeemable cost
of his invention, his fatigue. The eye
closes, and no other takes its place.
It is the end of god, each time, each time.

Yet, though the leaves must fall, the galaxies
rattle, detach, and fall, each to his own
perplexed and individual death, Lady Yang
gone with the inkberry's vermilion stalk,
the peony face behind a fan of frost,
the blue-moon eyebrow behind a fan of rain,
beyond recall by any alchemist
or incantation from the Book of Change:
unresumable, as, on Sheepfold Hill,
the fir cone of a thousand years ago:
still, in the loving, and the saying so,
as when we name the hill, and, with the name,
bestow an essence, and a meaning, too:
do we endow them with our lives?
                              They move

into another orbit: into a time
not theirs: and we become the bell to speak
this time: as we become new eyes
with which they see, the voice
in which they find duration, short or long,
the chthonic and hermetic song.
                              Beyond Sheepfold Hill,
gunshot again, the bird flies forth to meet
predestined death, to look with conscious sight
into the eye of light
the light unflinching that understands and loves.
And Sheepfold Hill accepts them, and is still.

The landscape and the language are the same.
And we ourselves are language and are land,
together grew with Sheepfold Hill, rock, and hand,
and mind, all taking substance in a thought
wrought out of mystery: birdflight and air
predestined from the first to be a pair:
as, in the atom, the living rhyme
invented her divisions, which in time,
and in the terms of time, would make and break
the text, the texture, and then all remake.
This powerful mind that can by thinking take
the order of the world and all remake,
will it, for joy in breaking, break instead
its own deep thought that thought itself be dead?
Already in our coil of rock and hand,
hidden in the cloud of mind, burning, fading,
under the waters, in the eyes of sand,
was that which in its time would understand.
Already in the Kingdom of the Dead
the scrolls were waiting for the names and dates
and what would there irrevocably be said.
The brush was in the hand, the poem was in the love,
the praise was in the word. The 'Book of Lives'

listed the name, Li Po, as an Immortal;
and it was time to travel. Not, this year,
north to the Damask City, or the Gorge,
but, by the phoenix borne, swift as the wind,
to the Jade Palace Portal. There
look through the clouded to the clear
and there watch evil like a brush-stroke disappear
in the last perfect rhyme
of the begin-all-end-all poem, time.

XII

Northwest by north. The grasshopper weathervane
bares to the moon his golden breastplate, swings
in his predicted circle, gilded legs and wings
bright with frost, predicting frost. The tide
scales with moon-silver, floods the marsh, fulfils
Payne Creek and Quivett Creek, rises to lift
the fishing-boats against a jetty wall;
and past them floods the plankton and the weed
and limp sea-lettuce for the horseshoe crab
who sleeps till daybreak in his nest of reed.
The hour is open as the mind is open.
Closed as the mind is closed. Opens as the hand opens
to receive the ghostly snowflakes of the moon, closes
to feel the sunbeams of the bloodstream warm
our human inheritance of touch. The air tonight
brings back, to the all-remembering world, its ghosts,
borne from the Great Year on the Wind Wheel Circle.
On that invisible wave we lift, we too,
and drag at secret moorings,
stirred by the ancient currents that gave us birth.

And they are here, Li Po and all the others,
our fathers and our mothers: the dead leaf's footstep

touches the grass: those who were lost at sea
and those the innocents the too-soon dead:

                    all mankind

and all it ever knew is here in-gathered,
held in our hands, and in the wind
breathed by the pines on Sheepfold Hill.

                  How still

the Quaker Graveyard, the Meeting House how still,
where Cousin Abiel, on a night like this,
now long since dead, but then how young, how young,
scuffing among the dead leaves after frost
looked up and saw the Wine Star, listened and heard
borne from all quarters the Wind Wheel Circle word:
the father within him, the mother within him, the self
coming to self through love of each for each.
In this small mute democracy of stones
is it Abiel or Li Po who lies
and lends us against death our speech?
They are the same, and it is both who teach.
The poets and the prophecies are ours:
and these are with us as we turn, in turn,
the leaves of love that fill the Book of Change.

2

Waynesburg College Library
Waynesburg, Pa.

# THE LOGOS IN FIFTH AVENUE

I

September, and Fifth Avenue, you said,
and said it somehow as if we both were dead:
and then as in an afterthought you said
'The first word on the tongue is it of love
and is our language, then, all love, each word
a kind of kindness, a kind of blessing?
                                    The heart, therefore,
was named the heart because we love the heart?
Or was it that the heart became the word?'
It is absurd: we look for meaning, find
that we are lost in an algebraic surd.
The hurricane between us, or, in the morning press,
reports of changes in the style of dress,
the breastless female or the sexless male—
o god but how our history grows stale
if it is this we come to at the end
of god's beginning! Anguish, did you say?
Anguish unjust? God's anguish?
                                    Play, play
the juke-box tunes of this unpopular day
the give-away and the say-hay-hay
forget the blind-man tapping with his cane
who will not see the autumn blue again

the newsboy with wet papers in the rain
the Big Board with its loss or gain:
excuse, or try to exorcise, the pain,
the anguish will remain.

      As it should do,
as it should do. What would we be
if when the wind blows we
were not, and always, broken with the tree
the christ in us so broken?

       What would we do
for fourth or fifth or heaventh avenue
and not with hope of recompense
or vanity of munificence
but with humility, and true?
Here is the locust tree, you see the thorns
it is the tree the tempest murdered, see
the starveling leaves stifled with soot
and suffer with the root
cramped under stinking asphalt!

      Come away
for we have front row seats at the latest play,
The Lilies of Gomorrah, The Bells of Sodom,
and we will save our sorrows till tomorrow.

## II

*Knock knock: knock knock: ring ring:*
what will the morning postman bring?
Sufficient unto the day the bills thereof
no valentine no harbinger of love
no mockingbird upon the video tree
to promise us the spring

                        yet let him sing
above the neon lights in Ptomaine Row
sing for the library sing for the jail
yes and for all our lights that fail
as now they do. And we'll sing too
sing for the things we meant to do and be
the sunrise that we could not wake to see
the alms we did not give

                    and the dear secret
found once, in the four-leafed clover, long since lost,
forgotten, or dissembled, or betrayed.

III

                              And now
take off the tarnished sock and go to bed
as if again we both were somehow dead
but as a prayer a remembered fraud of prayer
remember what you said.

                              What did I say?
Save it for another day.

                              What did I say?
Something of language, and of love, remember?
And something of September.

                              I did not say,
I merely asked. Asking is all we seem
as in a waking dream
to be able or partly able
to do. We wait for knockings on a table

                              which when they come
are random false or meaningless or dull.

                              Better to knock on wood
as someone said!

                              And did he mean a tree?
Better to go to bed and *scream*
when nightmare rears its eyeless head
from the mythic waters of sleep.

                              Better to keep

even in sleep as now you do
the something that you said you thought was true
the something borrowed with something *blue*.
                              And yes,
blue was for the blind-man, blue was for the sky,
blue was for the eye—
                    *I am not I.*

IV

Morning empties the garbage pails of night
morning empties the sky of clouds the mind of dreams
and see, the dapple-grey coursers of the sun
beat up the dawn with their bright silver hooves.
It was not I who said this, was not you,
and yet we know it true.
                              For the dream kept,
as the dream always does, while still you slept,
under the quilt and under the guilt
and the starless waters of sleep,
what we could not endure and not forget
the perdurable time
which, as the telltale dream admits,
is of the nature of a crime.
                              Listen:
a bell unthinking in unthinking sky
mocks the resentful ear, as at the eye
teases the minatory light of morning.
                              Wake!
and face reality once more, reality
which in its finite wisdom permits us each to die
but will not die itself!
                              Return

out of the flight of dream to face
the fever and the fret, the sad St. Vitus
dance of the hours, the god's and ours,
amid the drear detritus
that blows along the one-way street
                while at the corner
waits by the silver-wreathèd Cadillac
the undertaker's shiny black
                sole mourner
for someone's Little Boy Blue or lost Jack Horner
and the meek body that was his share of god.
             Today
we will again be circumspect
we know what to expect
the iceman with his fifty pounds of ice
nuns in a flutter at the convent door
              the scattered rice
left for the pigeons from the wedding-day
and fifty sample bedrooms to inspect.
And in those fifty bedrooms who will sleep
as we this night or keep
vigil even in dream?
             The tugboats mourn
in immemorial weather, the southeast wind
brings from the harbor rain, the clang
of ashcans rings on asphalt
            but our dream our dream
with a timepiece precision seems to keep
its tiny tick of truth.
            Take out your chalk

and on the sidewalk as for hopscotch mark
the humble squares for devious progress: not
as in our childhood blossom root or leaf
nor rich man poor man beggarman thief
but drugstore movie bar and car
garage post office hospital morgue
subway and comfort station. Shall we play?
in this poor hierarchy find our way?
Listen to what they say: 'Gee mom my tongue is dirty.'
'How can it be? It's in your mouth.'

        Or, 'Don't be stupid, kid,
dogs can't chew gum.'

        Better to pray
remembering what you said.

        What did I say?
And that was yesterday!

        Better today
to take a taxi up Fifth Avenue
visit the sealions at the Zoo
stop for a beer at the Shamrock Bar and see
a baseball game or prizefight on TV.

V

The siren wails, but not from the far islands,
nor for divine Ulysses, but down the street
to fire or death. The bent cat in the alley
slinks his despair. Under the tree of heaven
cheep-cheep cheep-cheep the dusty sparrows
forage for gravel.
                        On his stoop the priest
blank-faced now takes the air
an interval of blankness between prayer
intonements for atonement without meaning.
But you too something said of prayer.
                        I did not say of prayer
but as a remembered fraud of prayer
ritual of beseeching from childhood's teaching.
Yet it was true if as a reaching
of mind and hand to understand beyond
what we were taught as true and, yes, still true.
                        And is still true, for you?
Still true, but in a different way.
                        What did you say?
What was it that you said and took to bed
so that we dreamed it both and loved it both
yes loved it knee to knee the I becoming we?

41

44046

                         I said
each face of all we meet will soon be dead
I said the child is father to the corpse
I said the skeleton is in the womb
I said the city is a honeycomb
a honeycomb of tomb and there we move
or think we move who are already still
and there we love or think we love
                         and yet
perhaps we should not emphasize alone
the brevity of life the levity of stone.
Though this cathedral mausoleum fall
                         as fall it must and come to dust
and with its splendors us
                         still let us not forget
the nowness of the hand upon the bough,
the nowness of the now.
The living moment of the dream
with its timepiece precision watching truth
still keeps eternal youth
not only in the solar month and year
but always, and forever, here.
                         Stay, stay,
the hand upon the bough upon the heart
stand still o love o living art
that in the blood and in the sap and in the sun
as in our mythic dream last night
bids all remain unchanged:
urge now your love for all things demiurge
for that is he and that is we
and bid this pattern be.                    42

3

A IS FOR ALPHA : ALPHA IS FOR A

I

Now it begins. Now the subaqueous evening
exemplary as the inalterable moon
begins again to begin. With slight starts
of organ-grinder music (if the scene
is of city) or of—'*dee-dee-dee—!*'
chickadee trill if (as it is) it is country.
The shadow, complex, seven-branched, of the ancient lyre-tree
prolongs itself on the sensual lawn and fades away
predicting a reverse shadow at daybreak. The star
(for look, love, there is a star)
trills through the sunset like a bird
diamond point in crimson word
and melts, and we are heard.
So, now, the casual evening begins, and its slow texture
weaves us into a casuistry. We, who were just now thoughtless,
or lost in a loss of thought,
come to a breaking and dissolving
sunset of our own. The world ends
and another begins. The love ends
—or does it?—
and another begins. But the light
lasts forever, there is no night.

The hands you lift are sunset, and the hands
are the exemplary moon. The eyes you lift
change with the texture of the evening,
Venus it might be one way, Sirius the other;
the lengthening shadow, so intricate, so various, of the lyre-tree
prolongs our listening nerves into the coming light
of tomorrow. My love, observe a moon
unobserved by any till now. Bland and bleak
as any lovestruck human. Such as we?
Such as we. We are the silver rind
of moonlight, for now it hardens, now is crystal,
on this tree, this virgin locust tree, and we
are moon and tree.

Fade, fade, all into darkness fade,
but also into light
since one the other closes.
The texture of the evening is of roses,
and we are, for the moment, roses too.
Love is not much: it is a touch: but it is true.

Evening, which evens all things. Hand in hand
brindled by sunset thought we stand
prolonging our nerves, and with them nature, into another day.
We are the sacred players and the play:
we are the music, and what the musicians say:
and always our new title is Today.
Today, and yesterday; the divine dance
moves under heart and heaven, the wave of light
gathers its all for a breaking of time
and then falls inward. We are the rhyme
paired like two words in love, and move
in the twinned discord of a chord, our love
hidden in its own secret, like the rose.
Will the rose unclose, disclose?
finding—how naturally!—a reason for season?
It is ourselves that open, even
to the innermost heaven.
It is ourselves magically disguised
as harp-string and harp-song, birdsong and petal,
ice-metal, rain-metal,
ourselves curving the air with a wing
ourselves the air for the wing to find and follow
ourselves the sunlight and the swallow.

Divisibly indivisible we sing
the begin-all-end-all thing:
night becomes a god, and we the night,
for the unfolding and enfolding of our delight.

III

Intervals and interstices of texture
enthrall us, bring us to a standstill, bemuse
fingertip and eyebeam, idea and eye;
while the mind fills with wonders. The voice
is of what? Who said to it, 'rejoice'?
You there, I here; you with your mountains of snow,
and your seven golden seas, and the woven Nile,
and the sky piled high with purple clouds;
and I with my rocky Sahara, ribbed with lapis lazuli,
and the last sail melting into sunset:
these are the language of interval, the interstices
subtle and gigantic, unfathomable, inaudible,
hieroglyphic and hieratic, by which we speak.
The exchange is golden. It is thesaurus. The exchange
beggars us only then to endow us again,
exhausts us only to replenish. The simple rain
walking before us down the country lane
shuttling before us down the country lane
says it with silver, syllables it slowly,
repeats its holy, holy,
and into it, and into night,
we weave this love, this light.

4

# THE RETURN

Dear tiger lily, fanged and striped! you are the bravest,
you as well as another will serve to chant
tongued with flame our vernal madrigal,
sowing among sequins of last year's locust
love's golden rhetoric:
you and the celandine
of immaculate green.
Wraiths of snow run from the stallion sun,
quicksilver lizards of water
flick their tails into cisterns,
and on the tarnished grass
where north wind sheered his drifts
in phantom edifice
melts the last sickle of pale ice:
and there, in a little while, where late was snow
the Indian Pipes will blow.
O darling, listen—from the orchised bog
chuckles the ancient and omniscient frog
his gross venereal hymn:
and the reed-scented wind, the bulrush-rattling wind,
dreams like memory through the mind.
Now love returns once more, our lost and antique love,
dear tiger lily! above

the sad detritus of death:
fling we then out of doors and into hearts,
where the year freshly starts,
and join the song-sparrow
in Hymen's favorite song:
for treason late and long,
yes, the sly shibboleth
of treason to death, and love, and another season!

The oak leaves rustle in the thicket,
loosen themselves, detach, and fall,
pale brown, pale purple, harsh still;
the hawk hangs over his beloved hill
as love hangs over the destined heart:
and once more joyfully we begin
the ancient dance of meet and part,
                              wherein
each is in turn the hawk and each the heart.
We touch and meet, we touch and greet,
kiss gravely, tread apart,
next glance, and eye askance,
curtsey in courtship's bashful dance,
retreat, and then advance.
O unknown love
unknown and treacherous as that sky above
and as my own heart is,
what is the meaning of your kiss?
Each lover asks and answers this
in blinded bliss.

Glad, glad, the sound
of two hearts beating, together bound,
O but tumultuous the rest
of your face, love, that rests upon my breast,
tumultuous the rest
of each upon the other resting:
two worlds at war we are,
star dancing against star.

For each must learn in each
all the dark-rooted language under speech:
here, look! new love, the roots we did not know,
strong stems, deep stains, rich glories never guessed:
disparate origins and desperate sins,
acknowledged or unacknowledged, understood
or misunderstood; the labyrinthine windings
through the lewd galleries of the mind, to find
something or nothing; illusory findings
which vanish at the touch, or on exposure to the air,
and of which, only in default, are we aware;
hatred derived from love, love from terror,
the roots not knowing their own fruits;
the unpracticed, and then the all-too-practiced vices,
deliberate dishonesties and rehearsed voices;
purpose becoming mean, meanness purpose,
wants promoted to obsessions, and the obsessions
near to madness. Who am I, who are you,
that one to the other must be true, untrue,
or dissect untrue from true?
Who shall possess, or be possessed? possession
of how much? of what ecstasy, or for what duration?
Where, too, and in what characters shall we meet

playing what parts of the multitude we have played
wearing what masks and shabby costumes
on the strewn stage of habit? The attitudes
are predictable, and therefor false, they belong
to another situation, are the inheritance
of other loves and lusts. What beatitudes
can the wingèd god invoke from these? In what divine dance
instruct these stained and stinking puppets?
Out of such mouths what song, what song?

And yet the tiger lily, under the snow,
heedless alike of year ago or long ago,
and the endless history of her repeated love,
dares yet again to thrust above
the sad detritus of death, and grow:
and speaks with the song-sparrow the sly shibboleth
of another season, another treason!
Lost memory, lost love, lost to return,
can we, too, not be brave like these, relearn
O as if all were virginal and new
the hawk and heart of 'I' and 'You'?
O daring darling, can we not trust
once more that innocent sky
once more to break our hearts and die?

Comes now, comes she!
comes the unknown, the unpredictable,
she who is half spring, half summer,
between the lilac and the wrinkled apple blossom,
the unknown, all-unimagined newcomer,
birch foot, beech heart, myrtle hand,
and the indecipherable mind
and virgin bosom
and windflower grace
and timeless Etruscan pace
and the tiger's heart, cruel to be kind:
comes like the sunshot southwest wind
bidding the elm bough, soliciting
the fan of iris under the snow
for one more spring, one more spring:
while the hawk's wing
sickles the white-blossoming hill
with shadow of death, the scythe's shadow
shadowing the redwing into the meadow.
O innocence in guilt, and guilt in innocence,
she stoops, she hovers,
fiercest and subtlest, and yes, tenderest of lovers,
the ruthless one
whose eye is in the sun.

5

THE WALK IN THE GARDEN

I

Noting in slow sequence by waterclock of rain
or dandelion clock of sun
the green hours of trees and white hours of flowers:
annotating again the 'flower-glory of the season,
a book that is never done,' never done:
savoring phrases of green-white, mock-white,
while the ancient lyre-tree, the ancient plum,
adds for another May its solar sum
in silent galaxies of bloom:
it is here, interpreting these, translating these,
stopping in the morning to study these,
touching affectionately the cold bark
of the seven-branched tree, where bees
stir the stars and scatter them down:
it is here, in these whitenesses of thought,
poring over these pages of white thought,
that we ponder anew the lifelong miracle:
the miracle that in these we best remember,
and in wisdom treasure best,
the lost snows of another December,
and the lost heart, and the lost love.
What matter that we are older, that we age?
Blest that we live this morning, blest
that still we read the immortal book
and in time's sunlight turn another page.

Shall we call it, then, the walk in the garden?
the morning walk in the simple garden? But only if by this we mean
everything! The vast daybreak ascends the stairs of pale silver
above a murmur of acacias, the white crowns
shake dark and bright against that swift escalation of light,
and then, in intricate succession, the unfolding minutes and hours
are marked off by the slow and secret transactions
of ant and grassblade, mole and tree-root,
the shivering cascade of the cicada's downward cry, the visitation
(when the brazen noon invites) of that lightninged prism
the hummingbird, or the motionless hawkmoth.
Listen! The waterclock of sap in bough and bole,
in bud and twig, even in the dying
branch of the ancient plum-tree, this you hear, and clearly,
at eleven, or three, as the rusted rose-petal
drops softly, being bidden to do so, at the foot of the stem,
past the toad's unwinking eye! Call it
the voyage in the garden, too, for so it is:
the long voyage home, past cape and headland
of the forgotten or remembered: the mystic signal
is barely guessed in the spiderwort's golden eye, recognized
tardily, obscurely, in the quick bronze flash
from the little raindrop left to wither
in the hollow of a dead leaf, or a green fork
of celandine. For in this walk, this voyage,

it is yourself, the profound history of your 'self,'
that now as always you encounter. At eleven or three
it was past these folded capes and headlands, these decisions or refusals,
these little loves, or great,
that you once came. Did you love? did you hate?
did you murder, or refrain from murder, on an afternoon
of innocent cirrus in April? It is all recorded
(and with it man's history also)
in the garden syllables of dust and dew:
the crucifixions and betrayals,
the lying affirmations and conniving denials,
the cowardly assumptions, when you dared not face yourself,
the little deaths, and the great. Today
among these voluntary resumptions you walk a little way
toward tomorrow. What, then, will you choose to love or hate?
These leaves, these ants, these dews, these steadfast trifles, dictate
whether that further walk be little or great.
These waiting histories will have their say.

Waynesburg College Library
Waynesburg, Pa.

III

But of those other trifles, the too intrusive,
the factual, the actual, that are too intrusive,
too near, too close, too gross, for deeper meaning:
what of these, what will memory make of these?
Will these too yield in time to the magic of translation?
The bobby-pins, the daily news, the paper-clips, even
the stuffed two-headed calf once seen in a pawnshop window;
as indeed also the crumpled letter, furtively
dropped in the ashcan at the corner,
yes, and the torn half of the movie ticket, bright pink,
found inadvertently in the breast-pocket, to remind you—
but meanly—of other days of afternoon rain:
how will you profitably rehearse these,
how will you (otherwise than here!) rehearse these, and to what end
of reconstruction? for what inspired reinterpretation
of the lost image, the lost touch?
Useless, here, the immediate, the factual, the actual:
the telephone remains silent when most you wish to hear it:
the May morning, or is it August or September,
remains empty, infertile, at precisely that instant
when your heart—if that is what you mean by heart—
would invoke a vision.

                    Blessing enough, indeed, it might have been,
but not under peach-tree or lyre-tree,
in the persistence of the radio's tremolo
and the listening silence of an empty room:
blessing enough if in these should quietly have spoken,
in answer to that invocation, the not-voice of voice,
the now almost unknown and unfamiliar voice,
the voice at first not recognized when heard:
blessing enough if in these
indifferent accidents and meaningless impromptus
the angelic not-you should open the door
and angelically enter, to take slow possession
of the room, the chairs, the walls, the windows,
the open piano with its waiting keys,
and the poor bed under the forgotten picture,
but possessing also
the divine touch that in the radiant fingertips
could at once create, with a magician's eloquence,
nothing from something, or something from nothing:
as, out of the untouched piano,
a shabby chord, a threadbare tune, the banal air
squealing from the midnight juke-box, where,
at the corner saloon, over the tepid beer,
you sit and stare,
remembering how the days have become years,
and the minutes hours,
and the false sunlight is distilled to tears
in the sentimental involutions of a shared sound:
yes, and the touch of the fingertip, once, on the back of the hand,
or, for a braver instant, tentatively, along the line of the cheek:

but no, these are all a broken imagination only,
the one and only heart remains lonely,
the morning remains silent, cannot speak,
muted by the ridiculous trifles, the preposterous trifles,
that stammer between the past and you.
Only, in the thinking hands, for a moment,
the persistent stupid bloodstream vaguely traces—
as if on air, as if on air—
the lost touch, the lost image, the chimerical future:
praying, now, for the illusion of an abstract love.

IV

The illusion of an abstract love? Say, rather,
it was the loves and hates that were illusion,
and all that accompanied them: items of fatigue
or of dubious regret, denials and acceptances,
these it is that are as clouds
gone deathward over the morning, lost, dislimned,
and now recoverable only, if at all,
in the remembered crevice in the remembered garden wall:
abstracted out of space, abstracted out of time,
but now reset, by the morning walk in the garden,
in crystal rhyme.
In these rich leaves, which are not only leaves
of lyre-tree or pomecitron, but also leaves
of a living book that is never done:
from winter to summer, from spring to fall:
in these we keep them all.
Here is that abstract love which we would find
wherein all things become imperishable mind:
the numberless becomes one, the brief becomes everlasting,
the everlasting opens to close
in the perishing of the raindrop on the rose:
violence is understood, and at last still,
evil is fixed and quiet as a tree or hill,
but all alike acceptable and one
and in one pattern made to move, or not to move,

by the illusion, if it is illusion,
of an abstract love.
Touch now again the serpent skin of the lyre-tree:
stoop now again, a hummingbird,
to the magic of the mock-orange:
count again by waterclock of rain
or dandelion clock of sun
the slow days of trees, the quick hours of flowers:
this time, this matin-song, this love, is yours, is ours,
a book that is never done, never done.

OVERTURE TO TODAY

I

This day is not as other days: will not be
a pale and stencilled pattern of those others:
the golden nexus of the dream
from which you woke at six in a thrill of rain
the golden wall from which an unknown woman leaned and spoke
calling your name, and then
put forth her hand to touch your face
saying. 'This day
will not be as those others, come, we will go away
into another world, another city, where
each avenue will be light, each house a prayer
and song the equivalent of breath!'
                              Fair, fair,
shines in the dream the dream's unfolding
from be to seem
from chaos into shape
from fear from death
yet with at first what slow and leaden step
we strive towards the wings of our escape
into that other country, where,
caught in a rarer pattern of intent,
we draw an exquisite and conscious breath!

                    Design,
as in the intricate dream, in us is woven:
and like the multiple meaning of the dream
which changes as it gleams, we too
are ravelled out in fiery threads:
under the very mind's-eye reappear
the thousand faces and the thousand eyes,
in every facet of the hour,
with which ourselves ourselves surprise.
                    Seed to flower:
and flower to seed. The hourglass turns
and pours its golden grains. The animal lives
mysteriously to himself, ordained, inviolable,
in a compulsive dream. The human child
so lives too without knowing,
innocent, living at one with the earth, the mother,
innocent participant of death and birth
and of begetting. Yet he must wake
and in the moment of his waking take
terrible knowledge of the miracle that is self.
See how he stands enringed
by the angelic and demonic powers, the winged
and fanged and finned and clawed!
And awed, and overawed,
now fades his song of innocence
                    and now begins
anthem of earth and heaven,
a new and richer counterpoint of praise,
that with experience is given:
henceforward he can sing

a fairer thing:
the radiant mysteries
that now are shared, and his.

       Profound, profound,
celestial, or underground, or truly found
even in the hand's sore breadth, and the eye's beam,
as in the golden nexus of the dream,
the god of order like a golden worm
working in all things to his perfect term:
the golden rivet, reason, manifest
but only to our simple eyes in simplest form:
the mysteries
mostly impenetrable except in these, as these:
the pure simplicity of the flower
the little flower for the first time seen
above her shadow in her transparency of hour:
time taking transient shape in this, as time
takes shape in us who see
and in the foreforged word and chthonic rhyme
with which we bid it pause and be.
Who would not worship at the heart, the tree?
       And we
who are the source of all delight and light
in which the meaning of the song stands still
are part and parcel of the mystery.

II

And so, this day is not as others: no day
repeats the others. Yet what it brings
out of the instant past in its succession
for you the palimpsest of a dream, for the wild rose
time to open or to close,
time for the dead leaf to be crystal in the brook
for the opening or the shutting of the book
time for the oak to add another druid ring,
time to explore, time to explain
precisely why at six o'clock in a throb of rain
the cry of the pure heart was caught in a dream
precisely why
in the child's round vowel of song, or in the bird's
sleepy roulade, or in a myth, or a rune of words,
or on the blackboard in the school
where calligraphic chalk unfolds
a geometric golden rule;
design and the designer are the same,
the namer is the name.
                            We who divine,
waking or sleeping, or in the manifold dream,
define, then redefine,
by rule of thumb or harmony of number

seeking tomorrow's validity in curve or line or cosine
and in the eye that measures or in the thought
that through its own closed finite world of sense
                           takes measured flight
and always starting over, every day
brought to a standstill by the same or a different doubt,
the imagination like a kite reeled in
and then again reeled out:
                           we who divine
divine ourselves, divine our own divinity
                           it is the examination
of godhead by godhead
                           the imagination
of that which it is to be divine.

III

Six o'clock. The tiger dream relinquishes
the traumatic heart. The tiger rain
claws at the windowpane

                    and before we sleep again
the bell strikes in the remembering heart
and as in a lightning-flash of time

                    we see
backward into the abyss of all we know and are.
Wings in the night fly left and right
swarm downward and away, and far,
only the cry of sky

                    floats upward, 'What am I?'
Yes, what am I? from what arriving? and into what
ascending or descending? The multiple dream
assembles its mythic fragments, like a kaleidoscope
clicks them into a pattern. We begin
to know, or think we know, to understand
or think we understand. Then sleep again.

IV

Before the unknown day which is to come
from east and past and earth and sky
arriving like the tumid tide that swells
under the precursive and magnetic moon
and bringing like the tide its ancient freight
of solar and human history, we wait
veiled in a hushed anticipation, conscious of the hour
and yet unconscious also since its power
not in the marker of the bell but in the swell
of tidal mystery without within
is ours as well as time's. In a pure state
of irresponsible expectancy, of pregnancy,
like those who wait to see
a theatre's curtain drawn and what is there to be,
we wait, and stare, and know
that this will be no ordinary show:
that something godlike here begins
                              and greater far
than our poor dream may have conception of:
                              and yet
it is ourselves who have conceived
and have believed
that what we see will be the work of love.
                              This day
will be the enacting of that foredoomed play.

And now the musicians of the heart begin
with heartbeat drum and flute of truth
and tender violin, begin
the sacred overture:

                     at first the pure
song of the child the song of innocence
and daybreak air

                       and then the sober prayer
and anthem of experience

                       mature and sure
with contrapuntal weavings in and out
of love and wonder, faith and doubt,

                       and last
the many-voiced hymn of wisdom,

                       in which the past
of innocence and experience become one
the end implicit in the beginning

                       but all one . . .
                       And now the sun
divides the curtains of the night; our play,
of which the title is Today, will be begun.


What will it be? We do not know. But it will say:
love is the action which brings forth the day,
whether of will to love or will to live:
the necromancer's genius which brings forth
the golden All from the golden Nothing.
Love is poetry, the god's recreation,
his joy in *fiat*, the world becoming word.
It is creation and recreation, two words in one,

the poem always just begun
and never done.

                    The world as word
this is the poem which the wise poet writes
in us and through us and around us writes
                      o and invites
all things created, and all things to come,
each to make tribute and contribution make
to what is never whole
                    or wholly heard.

7

ANOTHER LYCIDAS

I

Yet once more in the empty room review
the photomatic photo on the table
which years have faded but from which
still behind owlish glasses stubborn eyes
under an ancient hatbrim fix your own.
                              Which nevertheless are his
since it is at a camera that he gazes
there in the railway station, his own image
rounded in a lens in a curtained cubicle
while outside, along an echoing concourse,
passengers hurry for trains and trains depart
                              and overhead
the silent clock the electric clock
                              *sans* tick *sans* tock
with quivering hand pricks off another second
advancing for his life a last October.
                              Yet once more view
the silent face whose fierce regard for you
follows you like a conscience: stubborn, sober,
who after two martinis waits
and thus kills time till the opening of the gates.
What train it is he waits for we well know.

Leaving behind the evening suburbs it will go
south to the Islands and the pinewood Cape
where he was born, and grew, and knew
as if it were a legend learned by heart
each name each house each village, that ancient land
familiar to him as his face, the land
whence came with the ancestral name
inheritance of those steadfast eyes, the hand
salt-stung salt-harsh that for his forebears threw
the barbed harpoon or turned the wheel to windward
and kept it by the compass true.

II

Bequeathing us this gimcrack photo
as he himself would say *pictore ignoto*
for contemplation now that he is dead
bequeathing it by accident and not intent
yet speaking to us still and of that day:
what else would he have said or what else say?
                              The massive head
and proud mustachios are not in his regard
and it is not at these he stares
who midway in his life no longer cares
(nel mezzo del cammin di nostra vita)
for vanity of self: what there he sees
and with his vision frees
beyond the Islands and the ancestral seas
and the hall bedroom the humble furnished room
in which he lived until he died:
                             beyond all these
is what he sees he has himself become
and, with him, us: and further still
what, out of yeoman courage, country skill,
the ploughshare patience, the seafarer's will,
has come, as for the sailor homeward bound,
a change of course.

                    Profound:
and yet not so, since simple must to complex grow.
And he who as a boy trapped muskrats in the creek
or through snow-stippled poverty-grass
tramped to the ringing pond to fish through ice
or rolled the barrel in, to salt the pork,
or sawed and split the pine and oak
in the pale sweetgrass by the cedar swamp
under a harvest moon that rose again
to silhouette the weathervane
above the meetinghouse: and who would say
year after year when he returned
the 'frost is on the punkin',' or 'I know
clam chowders on the backs of kitchen stoves
that have been there for nigh a hundred years':
                              or in the slate-cold churchyard,
where now unmarked he lies, point out the stone
on which appear these words alone:
 'The Chinese woman, name unknown': then tell
her story, and a hundred others, which each house
bespoke for him along a mile of elm-tree-shaded road:
                              he who from this had grown
and all this wood-lot lore had known
and never had forgotten, nevertheless
with this rich knowledge also took
to Buenos Aires Cadiz and the rest
                              and Harvard too
his boyhood's book, the scholar's book,
the book that was his life. This was to be
his change of course. What his forefathers learned

                                                              88

of wisdom, courage, skill, on land or sea,
rounding the whalespout horn, or in a summer's 'tempest,'
or 'burning off' in spring or sanding down a bog
or making the strict entries in a log
beneath the swinging lamp, in a clear script
the latitude and longtitude: this now would change
and the sea-change reverse. Chapter and verse
replace the log, and ripened scholarship
the island packet and the blue-water ship.

III

Humility was in that furnished room
as in the furnished room that was his mind.
The glass of sharpened pencils on the table
the pencil-sharpener on the windowsill
a row of well-worn books upon a bench
some Spanish and some French
the page-proofs spread out to be worked upon
a few whodunits and a lexicon

in a top drawer
a flask of bourbon or the full-ripened corn
for those who *might* be to the manner born

behind a curtain
the neatly folded clothes on hangers hung
an old guitar somewhat unstrung
and in its leather case upon the shelf
the top hat now no longer worn

tarnished for certain
but much used in more prosperous days.

An 'aluminium' kettle
sat in the corner behind his chair, for tea,

beside it a red apple.
And the tea-leaves went down the W.C.

                    Evening, by the Esplanade.
Sunset brindles the bridge, the evening star
pierces the cirrus over Chestnut Hill
                    and we are still
asking the twilight question. Where shall it be:
tonight, tonight again, where shall it be?
                    Down 'Mulberry' Street
beckon the streetlights, and our feet
                    through rain or snow or sleet
once more in unison to eastward turn
not to Priapus Garden or to view
what the 'poast' says is 'plaid' today
                    but if burlesque be on
to the Old Howard, or the Tam or Nip
the Oyster House or Silver Dollar Bar
then to the Athens, there once more to meet
with Piston's whole-tone wit or Wheelwright's neat
while the martinis flow and clams are sweet
and he himself our morning star
until Apollo's taxi ploughs the dawn.

                              Who would not mourn
for such a Lycidas? He did not know
himself to sing or build the lofty rhyme
or so he would himself have said: and yet
this was not true: for in him grew
the poet's vision like a tree of light
                              and leaves of light
were in him as the gift of tongues
                              and he was of those few
who, as he heard, reshaped the Word,
and made the poem or the music true:
and he was generous with what he knew.
                              Lightly, lightly, November,
the third unknown by him, with sunshot gale
from the Great Cove or Follins Pond bring home
the hawk and heron: while we remember
                              the untold wealth he took
into the grave with him, the open book
that lies beneath the grass
of all he knew and was:

                              composed by him
with calligraphic hand and curious eye
the pencil point unhurried, fine,
unfolding still its classic line
and waiting still for us to see:
and, at the end, the signet signature, 'G.B.'

Death's but a progress, or so Whitehead says.
The infant dies to childhood the child to boy
the boy to youth the youth to man.
                                    Try as we can
if we should think to try or makeshift make
                                    we cannot take
one age into another. Life is a span
which like the bridge the link not knowing link
comes to an end in earth as it began.
                                    We cannot think
end and beginning all at once but only
in the broken beam of light recall
the instant prism in a recession of successions.
And it is only we, the living, who can see
in such another instant of successions
                                    the span of such a man.

This book was designed by John Begg,
set in Georgian type and printed on
Hamilton White Wove Text paper by
S. A. Jacobs at The Golden Eagle Press